FEAST OR FAMINE?

THE ENERGY FUTURE

BY FRANKLYN M. BRANLEY

FEAST OR FAMINE?

THE ENERGY FUTURE

FRANKLYN M. BRANLEY

Illustrated by HENRY ROTH

Thomas Y. Crowell   New York

Library of Congress Cataloging in Publication Data

Branley, Franklyn Mansfield, 1915-
Feast or famine?

Bibliography: p.
SUMMARY: Discusses changes in transportation,
housing, and life-styles which may be both desirable
and necessary to help reduce fossil-fuel consumption.
1. Power resources—Juvenile literature.
2. Energy conservation—Juvenile literature.
[1. Power resources.   2. Energy conservation]
I. Roth, Henry, 1933-   II. Title.
TJ163.23.B72   1980   333.79   79-7817
ISBN 0-690-04040-7
ISBN 0-690-04041-5 (lib. bdg.)

1 2 3 4 5 6 7 8 9 10
First Edition

CONTENTS

THE METRIC SYSTEM OF MEASUREMENT USES:
meters for length
grams for mass (weight at sea level)
liters for volume

TO CONVERT ENGLISH MEASUREMENTS TO METRIC,
OR METRIC TO ENGLISH:
1 inch = 2.54 centimeters
1 foot = 0.305 meters
1 yard = 0.914 meters
1 mile = 1.609 kilometers
1 pound = 0.454 kilograms
1 quart = 0.946 liter
1 centimeter = 0.3937 inch
1 meter = 39.37 inches
1 kilometer = 0.621 mile
1 gram = 0.035 ounce
1 kilogram = 2.20 pounds
1 liter = 1.06 quarts

1 FEAST OR FAMINE?

The way you live depends upon energy. Energy determines whether you walk or ride; it determines the clothing you wear (energy is needed to produce cloth and to run machines), the food you eat (energy is needed to plant, care for, and harvest crops), your entertainment and education. When there is a lot of cheap energy many products are available. The standard of living improves as more people have electricity, refrigerators, cars, better food, and healthier bodies free of many diseases. The twentieth century has been a period of cheap and abundant energy for much of the world. In the United States and other industrial countries such as England, Germany, Japan, and more recently Russia, factories have been able to make thousands of products at prices that are affordable. People have homes to live in, practically everyone who wants a car has one and can afford to run it.

At the close of the 1970's, the price of energy, that is, oil, went up. Suddenly people realized how much they depend on it. Costs to run factories have risen, and so products made in factories are more expensive. It costs more to fly in an airplane, to ride in a bus or train, to drive a car, and to send products by truck—and all because oil prices have zoomed.

Some people believe that the oil shortage is here to stay, and that prosperity will never return. They say that people must not hope to have a new home, or a car, nourishing food at every meal, color television, or higher education. They say that people must go back to "horse-and-buggy living," back to the way people used to live a century and more ago. Pessimists see a world in collapse. Cities will decay because people cannot easily get in and out— there will be no trains or buses. Electricity will be turned on only a few hours each day; water will be available only part of the time. High-rise apartment houses will be useless; they cannot be heated and elevators will work only occasionally.

Food will be available, though in limited supply, because trains fired by coal will operate and be able to transport it; and machines that use coal will harvest the crops and process the foods. We will go back to canned fruits and vegetables, for there will be no refrigerators—there is not enough electricity for them. There will be no more supermarket shopping by car. Getting food will be a family chore, using bikes and wagons. Hopefully, someone in the area will have a horse and wagon to help out with deliveries.

The living style will change in private houses. There will be no oil for the furnace. Heating will be by coal—when people are lucky enough to get some. Those who can do so will move to areas where winters are milder—the Sun Belt, northern Africa, and the northern part of South America. As in the city, private houses in the country will have electricity for only part of the day, and the amount will be rationed.

These pessimists are right. An energy famine would change the world. All of us would travel less; we would have less food and clothing, fewer comforts—much of our time would be spent in getting food and shelter to stay alive.

And, if the world continues to depend upon oil as its principal source of energy, there will be an energy famine. Sooner or later there will not be enough oil to "run the world."

Fortunately there are optimists who feel there will be no energy famine, but an energy feast in the twenty-first century—that there will be plenty of energy for everyone. They see the oil economy (a world where oil is the principal fuel) as a very brief period in the history of the world. And it is, for once oil is used up it cannot be replaced—and so the oil economy ends. These optimists believe that the long history of the world, for centuries and millennia, will be based upon an endless, continuously renewable supply of energy that will come from many sources, such as the sun and nuclear fusion. They see a hydrogen-electric world in which cars, trains, planes, trucks, and buses will be run by hydrogen or electricity. Houses will be heated by electricity, and by heat pumps run by electricity. Electricity for industry, factories, and homes will come from solar converters and tokamaks—devices that convert the energy released in nuclear fusion into electricity. The fuel for such an economy will be hydrogen—as endless as the oceans of the world.

Tremendous problems must be solved before such an economy is possible. But men and women have the ingenuity to solve them. People have a choice—they can choose to have an energy famine, which will occur if we do nothing, or an energy feast, which can be enjoyed only after great effort and dedication. The time to start is now.

2 ENERGY ALTERNATIVES: CARS

Several decades ago there was no fuel problem in the world, largely because there were fewer cars. Today, in the United States, more than 130 million cars, buses, and trucks roll along the 4 million miles of streets and highways that interconnect the country. Each year these vehicles burn up over 100 000 million gallons of gasoline.

A government survey reported that people in the United States spend over 20 percent of their income on transportation. Most of this is for cars, including automobile insurance, repairs to keep them operating, and gasoline and oil to keep them running. The drain upon the fuel reserves of the world is tremendous.

The number of cars and highways in other parts of the world has also grown rapidly. In Russia, for example, 350 000 cars were produced in 1970; in 1980 that number has grown to over 2 million. In the United States close to 10 million cars are produced every year. Presently, about 4 million Soviet citizens own cars; in the United States the figure is about 98 million. It's probably just as well that there are fewer cars in Russia, for there are not enough roads on which to put them. There are less than a million miles of highways, and most of the roads are not paved. They are full of holes and during spring thaws become deeply rutted. Nevertheless, the figures show that Russia, like the rest of the world, is increasing its production of cars. The most popular car in Russia is the Zhigulis, a small compact vehicle that gets good mileage. However, Russia is also building a large luxury car, the Gaz 14. Indications are that this car will continue to be developed for those few officials who can afford its high price.

European and Japanese car manufacturers have always made small cars. In fact, many of the small cars used in the United States are imported from Japan, Germany, Italy, England, and Sweden. Small cars get better mileage from each gallon of gasoline, which makes a big difference in a nation's fuel consumption. The federal government has said that by 1985 new cars must average at least 27½ miles per gallon (about 12 kilometers per liter). Several small, light cars get that mileage or more right now. In the past few years, the value of large cars has decreased rapidly. Their resale value is much lower than that of smaller used cars.

The greater number of cars will contribute more and more to the fossil-fuel drain. However, this proves no immediate problem in Russia. The country produces more oil than it consumes and exports oil to many European countries.

The world trend toward smaller and more efficient cars will ease the fuel situation, but it will not solve the problem. The time will come when the supply of gasoline will be restricted; there will not be enough for everyone, regardless of how much mileage a car may get.

When that happens, there will be several ways of coping. The obvious one is to reduce the number of cars. Instead of each family having two or three cars, it would be limited to one small car. This would change the life-style of many people, and, in some cases, it would cause hardship. People would protest strongly, and the country's economy would slump, for much of it is based upon the need for cars—the more cars, the better the economy.

CONTROLLING GASOLINE USAGE

Another solution is to raise prices; it would seem that people would use less gasoline if they had to pay more for it. However, there are indications that price makes little difference. In Italy, where prices increased almost 100 percent after the 1973 shortage, use dropped sharply at first. But after a month or two, the amount sold was as high as ever—people became accustomed to the higher prices. Steadily increasing prices in the United States have not reduced usage very much. On the contrary, the demand for gasoline is still too high. Each year there are more cars, and people continue to drive more than is necessary. Apparently, they will drive as long as gasoline is available, no matter what the cost.

Gasoline rationing is a possibility that's less drastic than eliminating cars. Each car owner receives coupons that allow him to buy a certain amount of gasoline. A person who needs a car to earn a living—a cab driver or salesman, for example—would receive more coupons than would the person who doesn't require a car to earn his livelihood.

The idea behind gasoline rationing is sound. But there are many problems involved in making the system work. One of them is the problem of counterfeit coupons; fake coupons are printed and sold on a "black market." Selfish people with a lot of money and little patriotism pay large amounts for the coupons, thus getting all the gas that they want. There will always be people who think the laws are not made for them. If they want gasoline, they'll get it—one way or another.

Another way of controlling gasoline usage is to make it harder to get. For example, reduce the number of gas stations, an idea that is not popular, especially with people who own stations. Or, keep all the stations operating, but selling gas only on alternate days, or only to cars with certain license plate numbers. This has been tried several times during severe gasoline shortages. Recently, cars with license plates ending in an odd number could buy gas on odd-numbered days; even-numbered plates could buy gas on even-numbered days. Also, the amount that could be bought was limited depending upon the gas in the tank or the supply that was available.

People drove their cars less, only when they really needed to, and they did not buy "gas guzzlers." They bought smaller and lighter cars that got better mileage.

Alternate-buying days produced mile-long lines of cars waiting to get to the gas pumps. People who went on long trips requiring more than a tankful of gas stored an extra supply in their trunks if they could get it. Several of these cars were in accidents, and explosions and fires resulted because the storage cans were not safe. Travel for pleasure decreased, and many restaurants and motels were forced to shut down.

Alternate-buying days are only a temporary solution. As soon as gas supplies increase, people drive as much as ever. Also, big luxury cars are still available, though less popular.

Gasoline shortages remind us strongly of something that each of us knows but doesn't think about—the workings of our country are based upon the automobile. Cars provide livings for millions of people—iron and coal miners, metalworkers, glass and plastic makers, chemists and fabric workers, assembly-line workers, engineers of all kinds, bankers, lawyers, insurance writers, gas-station owners, motel and restaurant workers. There are few people who are not affected by cars, one way or another. When cars stop running, the whole country slows down.

Gasoline engines run best at a certain speed—not too fast or too slow. Presently, there is a national speed limit of 88 kilometers per hour (55 miles per hour). It is an efficient speed—fast enough to get you there, yet slow enough to waste a minimum amount of gasoline. It takes about 15 percent more fuel to go 110 kph (which many cars are doing on superhighways) than to go 88 kph. Fifteen percent of the daily use of gasoline is 4½ million gallons. Although all cars are not on superhighways all the time, a large enough number are to make a daily saving of more than a million gallons entirely possible. The slower speed is also a safety factor. As soon as it went into effect, the number of fatal traffic accidents decreased. People who exceed the speed limit are committing a traffic violation; more important, however, they are wasting gasoline and endangering the lives of other people.

Cars should be driven only when necessary. Even then, they should carry several passengers. For example, those who must drive back and forth to work can form car pools. In some areas cars pay heavy tolls to use bridges and tunnels. The tolls are lowered when there are passengers in the car. High tolls encourage people to share rides or to use public transportation. Buses are often provided fast lanes so that they do not get delayed in traffic jams. People should be encouraged to leave their cars at home, and ride the bus; it saves both time and fuel.

There are over 100 million cars on the roads in the United States, and the total grows larger each year. Though some cars do go to the junkpile, each year 10 million new cars roll off the assembly lines.

The cars in the United States burn up more than 112 billion gallons of gasoline a year. A good number of them average only 10 or 12 miles per gallon, and many even less than that. Cars built in 1978 averaged 18 mpg; some got more and some a lot less. That was 34 percent better than cars built in 1974. By 1985 new cars will average 27½ mpg, and the average mileage for all cars on the road may be up to 20 miles per gallon. If so, there will be a yearly savings of 40 billion gallons of gasoline. (Throughout most of this book, we'll be using metric measurements. However, we start with gallons and miles per hour because that is the system still used in most newspapers and other media.)

Average miles per gallon can be increased, if Americans would get over their desire for big cars. Some say we never will. Americans are status-conscious, and one example of a status symbol is a big car. The way to end all this lies not in placing high taxes on luxury cars, which will probably be done, but in phasing them out of production. As long as gas guzzlers are available, there will be some people to buy them.

During the next several years, we must save billions of gallons of fuel. Cars must be made lighter and smaller. Driving speed must be regulated. Engines that make better use of gasoline must be developed.

ELECTRIC CARS

When cars throughout the world are small and light, and when they are driven in ways to save the most gasoline, they will still use billions of gallons of fuel every year. The gasoline comes from

An experimental solar electric car developed in Israel. Solar cells produce electricity, which is stored in batteries. The electricity drives the motor. *(Consulate General of Israel in New York)*

fossil fuels that will not last forever; they cannot be replaced. What will happen when there is no more gasoline?

According to some experts, gasohol (a mixture of gasoline and alcohol) will solve the problem. While it will stretch the gasoline reserves, alcohol cannot be produced in quantities large enough to replace gasoline. Others say electric cars will take the place of gasoline-powered cars. The electricity will be produced in generating stations that will use coal or nuclear fuel. Right now, there are a few small cars and delivery vans that operate on electricity. They carry several heavy batteries. At night the vehicle is plugged into any electrical outlet, and the batteries are charged. The electric charge is strong enough to push a small vehicle at slow speeds for several hours. Electric cars are not meant for highway travel; they are best suited for local driving, where distances are short and driving speed is slow. Battery-electric cars are being tested in many countries. In Israel test cars are equipped with solar-electric cells. The hood and roof are covered with these cells. The car is parked in full sunlight; sunlight generates electricity in the cells, and the electricity charges the batteries. The cars can travel only a short time before the batteries need recharging. The cost of the cells and such a vehicle's limited use will make it difficult to develop wide acceptance. It is more a novelty than a solution to the energy dilemma.

One of the main problems with electricity is storage. Electricity may be thought of more as a way of transporting energy than as energy itself. You can't put large amounts of electricity in a box and keep it for use later on, as you can with coal, oil, or gas. One way of "storing" electricity is to use batteries, of course; but the amount that can be stored in this way is small. Batteries are fine when the demand is modest. However, the number of batteries needed to provide a sizable amount of energy over an extended period of time limits their use.

HYDROGEN AS FUEL

There are engineers who think that hydrogen will replace oil (gasoline) as the principal fuel. The hydrogen will be obtained from the reaction of steam with coal, or from water as an electric current passes through it. The electricity can be generated by coal and nuclear generators: by falling water or the motion of the tides to generate hydroelectric power; by solar power for solar-electric cells; solar heat to generate steam; and heat from the earth (geothermal) to drive generators. And there are other ways: harnessing the wind and using the temperature difference between the surface of the oceans and the lower depths.

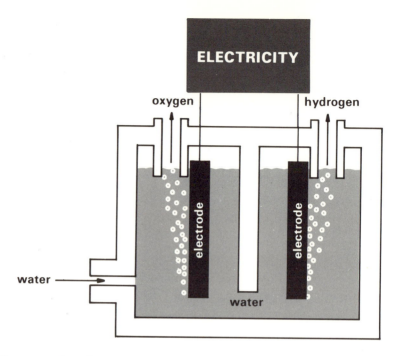

ELECTRICITY

oxygen   hydrogen

electrode   electrode

water

water

When an electric current passes through water, hydrogen and oxygen are produced. The process is called electrolysis.

When electricity passes through water, it separates the water molecule into hydrogen and oxygen. These gases can be stored, and large amounts can be compressed (liquefied) to occupy a small volume. However, hydrogen is highly explosive; it must be kept very cold and handled with care. The hydrogen can be made much more manageable by combining it with nitrogen in the air to produce ammonia (NH_3). Or it may be made into hydrides by combining the hydrogen with iron (iron hydride), or with titanium (titanium hydride). In this form, the hydrogen can be stored more safely. Though it is a safer method, it is not as efficient because it requires energy to combine the two gases, and it also requires energy to release the hydrogen when it is needed.

When the hydrogen is combined with oxygen, heat is generated, or electricity, as one wishes. When hydrogen and oxygen combine (when they burn) there are no polluting by-products. Water is the only substance that is formed.

The Brazilian and West German governments, as well as car and airplane companies in the United States, are encouraging research and development of pilot plants to produce hydrogen and engines to run on hydrogen. Brazil is in the tropical zone; thus, in addition, that country is developing solar generation of hydrogen.

Experimental cars are now operating that use hydride storage of hydrogen. The car carries a hydride tank; when it is refueled, hydrogen goes into the tank. Powdery iron and titanium take up the hydrogen. The metal particles become saturated, and small amounts of free hydrogen remain between the particles. This hydrogen is used to start the engine. The engine uses a slightly modified carburetor that mixes air with the hydrogen.

An experimental car that runs on hydrogen.

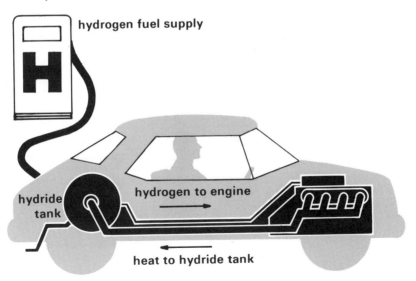

hydrogen fuel supply

hydride tank

hydrogen to engine

heat to hydride tank

Once it is running, the engine generates heat. Part of the heat goes to the hydride tank, where it causes the hydrides to release more hydrogen. Presently, the test cars get about a hundred miles to a fill-up. The tanks can be recharged in about half an hour (battery-electric cars take ten to twelve hours to be recharged). And the hydride tanks will not wear out; this is quite different from battery-electric cars, which must be fitted with new batteries every two years.

Hydrogen may also be used as the fuel in cars powered by electric fuel cells. A cell is a simple device consisting of three

One way hydrogen can be used is in fuel cells. When hydrogen and oxygen combine in the cell, electricity is produced. The waste product is water.

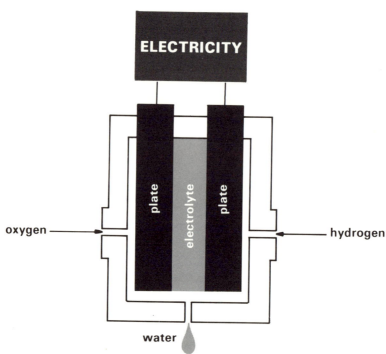

nonmoving parts: a fuel plate, an air or oxygen plate, and a conductor separating the two plates. When the plates are connected by an outside circuit, electricity flows from one plate to the other. In the process, water is formed. It is possible that fuel cells will become increasingly important as an energy source in the years ahead.

Research on hydrogen cars will continue as engineers seek ways to make them more efficient. When the cost of hydrogen is reduced, and when hydrogen is widely distributed (perhaps using the present gas pipelines), hydrogen engines may gradually replace gasoline engines.

It would seem that hydrogen is the fuel of the future. Maybe so. It is the most abundant substance in the universe; huge amounts are contained in coal deposits and in oceans and seas. As gasoline engines become obsolete, the development and production of hydrogen as a fuel should become very inexpensive, sparking a new era of prosperity.

3 ENERGY ALTERNATIVES: TRANSPORTATION

Although coal is plentiful, unless it is first changed to oil or gas, which is an expensive operation, it cannot be used in airplanes, cars, trucks, or buses. Coal can be used in industry, where its bulk and weight are no drawback; the oil that is saved could then be available for transportation. But even so, ways of living that do not demand massive amounts of coal and oil must be found. As was mentioned earlier, one obvious way is to reduce the number, size, and use of cars. Tremendous amounts of fuel can also be saved by reducing the number of buses, trucks, and airplanes.

SCHOOL BUSES

Many schools use buses to carry children back and forth every day of the school year. Our present educational system now requires

236 000 school buses; many of these buses are large and heavy, and get only six miles per gallon or less. Some people believe that by modifying the school system, the mileage covered by school buses can also be reduced.

In all likelihood, your school system uses a good many buses. It might be interesting to know just how many your school does have, or how many are actually operated by the system of which your school is a part.

Suppose your school has six buses that operate each school day. Also, let's suppose that the average distance traveled is 40 kilometers a day, making a total of 240 kilometers for the six buses. If the buses get 2 kilometers per liter (they probably get less), they would burn 120 liters of gas every day, 600 liters a week, or about 25 000 liters (6 000 gallons) a year.

There are at least 40 000 schools in the country that have school buses, and the buses carry some 22 000 000 children. Suppose averages are about like those used in the above example. The amount of gasoline used in the school buses of the country in each year comes close to 3.8 billion liters—1 billion gallons.

There are ways to reduce that number. In some areas buses are essential; we have made them so. But there are several locations where children who are now riding buses could walk to and from school. Those within three kilometers could, especially when they're in the upper grades. Sidewalks may have to be put down, but that can be done. (Incidentally, if more children walked, there would be an improvement in health statistics. Walking is the best of all exercises, and most of us, including children, don't walk enough.) Without causing hardship, it's reasonable to assume that the number of buses could be reduced by one-third; the saving in fuel would be about 1.1 billion liters—about 300 million gallons a year.

As fuel becomes more scarce, the busing question will not be a

17

matter of choice; the number of buses and the distances traveled will have to be reduced. Where the central school is too far away for children to walk, the school will have to move closer to the children. This can be accomplished through the development of cluster housing.

A single cluster is designed to provide housing for about a dozen families. In each cluster, the interior of one of the units is divided to make two or three classrooms that will serve the families in the cluster. (When not used for schoolchildren, the unit becomes a community center.) Children who live in the cluster are divided into two or three groups, according to age. Education becomes a community enterprise, a process in which each parent becomes involved. All children walk to and from school. There is no need for buses and no need for parents to taxi children back and forth.

Diagram of a cluster community.

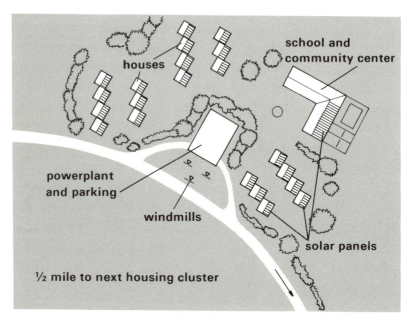

There's nothing new about this plan. In fact, a few generations ago most children in America walked to small community schools. There were no school buses.

Children attend a cluster school until about twelve years of age. They then transfer to a two-year middle school, which is in a larger building, but still an integral part of a cluster. It serves several clusters of homes, all within easy walking distance of a kilometer or two.

At the age of fifteen or sixteen, children go to boarding schools for a three-year period. This would complete formal education for many students.

A system such as the above would be possible even when there is little fuel for transportation. No doubt, there are drawbacks to it. However, many educators think that small, local schools are often more effective than large, central installations—and the total cost is less.

LOCAL TRAVEL

Cluster houses could be arranged so that a business cluster is located within two miles of any given group, making it easy to reach by walking or bicycling. The middle school mentioned above would be at the same location. A person would walk there for food shopping, let us say. Some of the purchases would be carried home; the bulk of them would be packed and delivered to the cluster within an hour or two. A small delivery van would make the rounds of a group of clusters at regular intervals.

A single light delivery van, using a minimum amount of fuel, could serve seventy or eighty families. Presently, each of these families drives a car, in many cases a gas-eater that weighs two tons or more. A person drives the car to the shopping center, parks the car, and drives home again, just to purchase a quart of milk.

In the cluster idea a person could shop via television and computer selection without leaving home. Within a few decades, people will not need to "go shopping." Products will be displayed by two-way television. Buyers will make selections using a small computer that connects through the television to a large computer. This will control machinery that puts the order together. Aspects of this kind of shopping are being practiced right now in experimental installations.

People who live in cluster houses would not require a car for most purposes. Recreation and education would be within walking distance. Each cluster might have a car pool, consisting of half a dozen cars that serve all people in the cluster. The cars would be used only when necessary, and not for hauling children to and from school, the tennis courts or swimming pool, baseball games, music lessons, or whatever. All would be within walking distance.

Huge cities would become smaller, and access to them would be by rapid transit. People in cluster houses would be transported to depots that serve the rapid transit line with trains similar to present subways, or in some cases monorails suspended above the old highway routes. The trains would be powered by electricity, and the electricity would be generated in fusion reactors.

AIR TRAVEL

Large airplanes burn 3 800 gallons of fuel an hour; the Concorde burns 7 000 gallons an hour. And this is so whether the planes are full or empty. (The average home owner burns 2 000 gallons of oil or less during an entire winter season.) Airline companies are able to make a good profit when their planes are 70 percent loaded.

However, many flights operate with only 50 percent, or less, of the seats occupied. If each plane carried 95 percent of its capacity, the number of planes in the air could be cut by almost 30 percent, with a similar saving in fuel.

Charter flights get around the problem of underloading. A flight is planned well ahead of time, and people who sign up for it can fly at a rate lower than a regularly scheduled flight. If a sufficient number of passengers is not booked, the flight is canceled. In the future, some form of chartering flights may be followed more widely.

People will also have to lower their expectations. In many parts of the country, if you want to fly from city to city, all you need do is go to the airport and get on a plane. In New York, for example, if you've just missed a plane for Chicago, another will take off in one hour. (And that's a single airline. During that hour, other airlines will also be sending planes to Chicago.) The same is true if you are taking a "shuttle" to Boston or Washington, D.C. Many of these planes are full, but a good many of them have space for many more passengers. The fuel consumption per passenger becomes much too high.

Theoretically, airplanes can be designed to go faster and faster, almost without limit. Jet engines can operate at high altitudes, but they need atmosphere in order to function—they cannot fly above it. Rockets, however, work best in outer space, where there is no atmosphere.

It is possible to design a jet-rocket passenger plane. Jets would take the plane to high altitudes, where the air is thin. At elevation the rockets would turn on and accelerate the plane to several thousand miles an hour. For landing, the plane would descend to the atmosphere and switch to the jet engines. A plane such as this would take only an hour or so to get from California to New York, or from New York to London. But the fuel expenditure would be

21

tremendous. (In a small rocket, one weighing about five tons, for example, four-fifths of that weight is fuel.)

Supersonic planes cover the route from the United States to Europe in three and one-half hours. But the fuel cost is 245 gallons per person, assuming there is a full load of 100 passengers. (A 747, which carries 360 passengers, has a fuel cost of about 65 gallons per person.) People must ask if the world can afford the luxury of such fast transportation as rocket-jets or supersonic passenger planes; is the time saved worth the fuel expended? The time will come when there will not be enough fossil fuel to power these supercraft. The answer then will be forced upon us.

FUEL AND DEFENSE

The armies of the world have thousands of ships, tanks, airplanes, rockets, and millions of trucks, tractors, bulldozers, and special vehicles that burn prodigious amounts of fuel and have made war a mobile, mechanized operation.

Every hour of every day, even in peacetime, many of these fuel-gulpers are operating. Bombers are in the air continuously around the clock. They can strike anywhere in the world in a matter of hours. (A bomber burns at least 3 000 gallons of fuel every hour.) Submarines carrying nuclear warhead rockets patrol the oceans of the world night and day, year in and year out. (They are usually powered by nuclear energy, however, and do not drain the fossil-fuel reserves).

Politicians must find ways to reduce the amount of armaments nations of the world need (or think they need) to defend themselves against attack. Right now, there is enough stored fuel to keep the war machines going. But fuel reserves will decrease. Tanks, planes, trucks, and ships will come to a dead stop when there is no fuel to operate them. Those countries that have fuel reserves will make demands upon those countries that do not. The world could become ruled by the oil-rich countries. We have already experienced their effect on our money supply. The OPEC countries (Organization of Petroleum Exporting Countries) have sharply increased the price of oil so that each year billions of dollars leave our country. In 1980 every driver paid—$20 or more to fill the gas tank, double what it was only a few years ago. And, very likely, the cost of filling the tank will rapidly rise to $50.

The government stores fuel for emergencies. Above-ground oil tanks and underground caves are located in well-protected areas. But there could never be enough tanks to hold the fuel needed to keep a war going, should one occur.

If there must be wars, military minds must think in terms of fuel-conserving wars. This may mean that superweapons will be used, weapons that will cause fast and total destruction. At the moment, we are not far from that kind of warfare. Right now, solid-fuel rockets with nuclear warheads are ready to be fired from land-based silos and from cruising submarines.

The race to produce the biggest bombs, the fastest planes, the most powerful tanks, the heaviest and fastest ships is nonsense. It drains the world of valuable resources. In 1980 the United States spent $60 million for defense every hour of a forty-hour work week. And the amount is increasing. There is no end to the race. Once in it, you can never win, because the "other side" will always build something a little faster, or more powerful, or more deadly. Perhaps, as some suggest, the decline in fossil fuels will have some positive implications, not the least of which may be a decline in the race for control of the earth.

When there are no more fossil fuels the war machines of the world will have to be powered by other kinds of fuel. Or people may finally realize that war is the great destroyer—there are no winners.

4 ENERGY ALTERNATIVES: HOUSES

In 1950 energy equal to about 160 million gallons of oil was needed every day to heat houses, office buildings, apartment houses, and public buildings such as schools and hospitals. By 1970 the need had grown to the equivalent of 315 million gallons. In 1985, when the population and living standards will be higher, the total needed will be even greater, probably more than 500 million gallons, unless steps are taken now to reduce the demand.

New houses and office buildings must be engineered to use the smallest possible amount of energy. Older structures must be improved wherever possible, so that they become more efficient.

In a recent survey made of suburban houses on a particular street, this is what was found: in 15 houses, some of them with 7 and 8 rooms, there lived 29 people. The total number of rooms in the 15 houses was 109. Obviously, the houses on this street are much larger than they have to be to provide good housing for the number of people involved. You might make a survey of your own area to find the average number of people in each house. You'll probably find that the houses have many more rooms than are necessary.

Many new houses are getting more and more lavish. Figures released by the Department of Commerce recently showed that two out of three of the houses built the previous year had two or more bathrooms, three out of five had fireplaces (which waste energy), and more than half of them had 1 600 square feet, or more, of living space. (A house with 1 600 square feet is a good-sized one. It might be interesting to find the number of square feet in your own house.)

CONSERVING HEAT

We imagine that in practically every house, each of the rooms is heated. To reduce the energy drain, each family must reduce the number of rooms that they need, and turn off the heat in those rooms. This can be done simply by closing the register, when heating is by hot air; if by hot water circulating through radiators, the pipes may have valves that can reduce the flow to a trickle, just enough to keep the water circulating. In some cases, the radiators can be drained and shut off.

All of us should get used to lower temperatures. When fuel was abundant and inexpensive, temperatures were kept between 70 and 72° F (21° C) in winter, even higher. People were careless about leaving doors open, and windows were not weatherproofed. Now, we must get used to colder houses; there is a savings of about 4 percent of fuel for every drop of one degree. We must set our thermostats at 18° C, which is warm enough except for the elderly and those who are ill. (You'll have to wear warmer clothing and snuggies, instead of skimpy underwear.) During the night the temperature can be 16° C; wool blankets will keep you warm. It's a bit chilly getting out from under the covers; but these lower temperatures will save millions of gallons of fuel every day.

In the evening, when people are less active, the 18° C temperature may be not quite comfortable enough. Instead of using the living room, a basement recreation room could become the center of activity. In many houses it's possible to build a room below ground level. Such rooms are easy to heat, and they are comfortable because heat does not escape easily; the cement walls and surrounding earth are good insulators. Also, there are fewer doors and windows through which heat can be lost. When family activities are centered in the basement area, thermostats in the rest of the house can be turned down earlier. Each hour of lower temperatures means a considerable saving in fuel consumption.

Heat escaping from a house shows up as white areas on infrared film. Places of greatest loss are the whitest. *(Owens-Corning Fiberglas Corporation)*

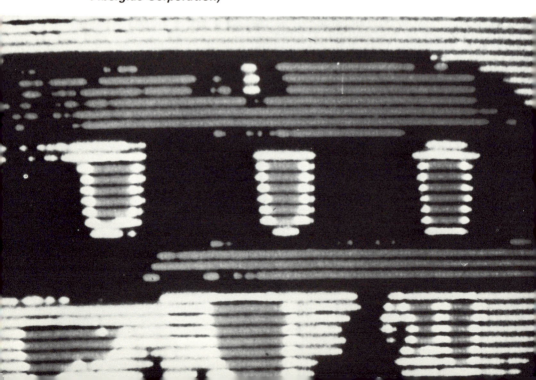

INSULATION

Lower temperatures save fuel, but much fuel is wasted because of excessive heat loss from our houses. Heat leaking from houses can be detected by infrared radiation. When cameras equipped with infrared film photograph a house, heat leaks are revealed. They are greatest around windows and doors. However, great amounts of heat also leak through the roof and walls of a house. They must be insulated with glass wool (or some equally effective material). The floor of the attic should have six inches of insulation laid between the timbers. In houses already built, insulating foam can be blown into the outside walls. Holes are cut, the material is blown in, and the openings are sealed.

Insulation is not cheap. However, fuel is a lot more expensive and will become even more so. The amount of money spent on insulation will be recovered in reduced fuel needs. In addition, your house will be more comfortable.

Doors and windows must be weather-stripped and cracks sealed. Also, storm windows and storm doors will act as barriers against heat loss. Windows with two panes of glass (double glazing) reduce loss; those with triple glazing are even more effective.

Many utility companies provide free or low-cost booklets that home owners can use to make a survey of their houses to find places where heat might be escaping. Some companies also have specialists who will come to your house. Then they suggest ways you can reduce heat loss and heat your house with less fuel. Such a service costs only about ten dollars.

The framework for the walls of houses is made of two-by-fours (timbers that measure two by four inches and run from floor to ceiling) that are spaced sixteen inches apart. The space between the inner and outer walls, which is four inches deep, is filled with blankets of insulating material. Electric wires may also be located in this same space, together with outlets and switches.

In order to get more insulation in the walls, many houses now being built use two-by-six studs instead of two-by-fours. The wider studs are stronger and can be spaced twenty-four inches apart. The walls, therefore, are six inches thick and so they contain six inches of insulation, which is a good deal more effective than the usual four inches. These houses, originally designed in the early 1960's, have other heat-saving features. Insulation in the ceiling is twelve inches thick instead of the usual six inches. There are fewer windows, especially on the north side, from which heat can escape. Even the basement is insulated, usually with sheets of styrofoam that are glued to the walls. Chimneys are located on inside walls so that some of their heat goes into the house. There are no wires or electric outlets inside the exterior walls to interfere with even distribution of the insulating material.

Windows and doors throughout are double-glazed. There is dead air space between the panes, which reduces the passage of heat. In winter many home owners cover the double-paned windows with storm windows, making three layers of glass.

Even when houses are completely insulated against heat loss, and windows and doors are treated so they lose the least amount of heat, much energy is needed to keep the building comfortable. The heat must come from one of the fossil fuels, unless other sources of energy are developed. One energy saver is a heat pump, a device that heats a house in the winter and cools it in the summer.

HOT WATER

Hot water is an expensive luxury of modern living. It takes a lot of heat (fuel) to raise the temperature of water. If flames were held under cups of steel pellets, aluminum pellets, and water, the metal would heat up long before the water. Water holds a lot of heat, which means it takes a lot of heat (fuel) to raise its temperature.

Each of us must learn to get along with less hot water, and to be content with a lower temperature. Take medium-warm showers instead of baths, and don't keep the shower running any longer than necessary.

Washing machines should be used only when there's a full load of wash to be done. And it's the same with dishwashers. If you must use them, run them only when the machine is full.

When only a quart or so of hot water is needed, don't turn on the faucet. It is much cheaper to heat the water on top of the stove. When you turn on the faucet for only a quart or so, much hot water is left in the pipes leading to the faucet; it is wasted.

PILOT LIGHTS

Many gas furnaces, water heaters, and stoves have pilot lights that burn continually, because it's not practical to ignite a furnace or water heater by hand. However, there are electric spark igniters for many of these appliances. When the thermostat calls for heat, a spark ignites the fuel, so there is no need for a pilot light that wastes a lot of fuel.

A hand-operated spark igniter is convenient for lighting the gas in a cook stove. There are set screws that can be turned to shut off pilot lights. When needed, a burner can be lit by simply turning on the appropriate burner and snapping a spark igniter over it. Millions of dollars worth of valuable gas could be saved if pilot lights were turned off. Many hesitate to do this because of the danger of gas leakage should a burner be turned on accidentally and not ignited right away. To eliminate this hazard, stoves should have locking valves that can be turned on only by performing a series of movements, such as pushing and turning, or depressing a release button and then turning.

ENERGY-ENGINEERED HOUSES

There are many ways we can save energy in our houses right now. When everyone is doing his or her best, our energy reserves will last a lot longer. But even so, the supply eventually will become critical. Not only must we conserve energy in our present homes, but we must design houses so that they require a minimum amount of energy, and develop other sources of energy. Also, we will have to change our way of living so it becomes less energy-dependent. Houses of the future must be smaller and energy efficient.

CENTRAL HEATING PLANTS

Instead of having a gas or oil furnace in each private house, it may be more efficient to have a central heating plant that serves a whole community. As new private homes are planned, attention must be given to clustering. How clustering affects schools has already been discussed in chapter three. In many parts of the country, houses are being built closer together and often are interconnected. Each cluster has a powerhouse that contains the equipment for heating the houses and for supplying hot water to the living units. It has been suggested that each cluster, or group of clusters, should also generate its own electricity. This may happen eventually, but right now it seems more efficient to operate a few large generators rather than several small ones.

The fuel presently used in these central heating boilers is oil. But they can be converted to use coal for at least the next several decades. Large coal furnaces can be engineered so they burn coal completely, thus reducing the amount of sulfur, ash, and other by-products of burning that pollute the air. This eliminates one of the main objections to the burning of coal.

HEAT PUMP

Your refrigerator is a heat exchanger. It removes heat from inside the box, making it colder, and puts the heat into the kitchen. The basic parts of a refrigerator are a compressor, an evaporator, and a radiator. The compressor changes a gaseous refrigerant, such as Freon, into a liquid. A refrigerant is a liquid that rapidly changes to a gas in the evaporator, which is inside the refrigerator. As it evaporates, the refrigerant cools quickly. Heat from the box flows to the cooled refrigerant, and the gas, which is now at a higher temperature, passes through a radiator that is outside the refrigerator. Here the refrigerant loses heat to the kitchen. The gaseous refrigerant is compressed into a liquid again, and the cycle is repeated.

A heat pump is a super-refrigerator that takes heat from the ground, or from the outside air, and transfers it into the house. Below the frost line, the temperature of the subsoil remains at about 13° C summer and winter. The evaporator of a heat pump, placed in a deep hole in the ground, takes heat from the earth. The refrigerant inside the evaporator is now heated. It passes through the radiator located inside the house, and there the heat is transferred to the house. A fan pushes the heat to the various rooms.

A compressor changes the refrigerant to a liquid, which then goes to the evaporator.

Instead of placing it in the ground, the evaporator could be located in the outside air on the outer wall of a building, for even cold air contains heat. (The only air, or other substance, that has no heat is that which has a temperature of absolute zero. That's 0° Kelvin, or −273° C. Anything warmer than that contains heat.) The heat pump collects heat, by way of the evaporator, from a large volume of outside air and puts it into the house. The pump concentrates the heat.

A more efficient heat pump is one that is solar-assisted. The evaporator is placed inside a solar heat collector. The collector traps solar energy; on a freezing day the temperature inside a collector might be 38° C or more. Since the evaporator is surrounded by warm air, evaporation and, therefore, heat collection occur rapidly. This reduces the running time of the system, which means that less electricity is needed for the compressor, the pumps, and the fans. A heat pump needs electricity to run the compressor, but it is cheaper to operate because it burns no fuel such as oil or coal.

AIR CONDITIONING

You would think that demand for fuels would drop in the summer. However, on hot, sultry days homes and public buildings, such as office buildings, hospitals, and restaurants, must be air-conditioned. The demand for electricity soars. In some cases, it becomes so high that the system breaks down, causing a brownout (partial loss of power) or a blackout (complete power loss).

One solution is to use the same highly efficient heat pump for cooling during the summer months. All one does is reverse the cycle. The radiator inside the house becomes the evaporator, and the evaporator located outside becomes the radiator. Heat from the house is collected in the evaporator. The heat is removed from the house and put outside, either in the ground or in the air, by way of the radiator. The ability to cool in summer is an important advantage of a heat pump. A single system heats and cools a house; thus installation costs are reduced. Operating costs are not excessively high, either, and they can be reduced by a method that recycles the energy.

CYCLED ENERGY

A house that uses a heat pump in a special way is being tested at the University of Tennessee in Knoxville. The system may cut the annual amount of electricity needed to heat and cool a house by 50 percent.

The unique part of the system is an insulated tank of water that serves as an energy-storage bin. For an average-sized house, a tank holding nearly 100 cubic meters of water is sufficient. It could be built into a cellar or installed under a driveway or patio.

Heat is taken from the water by the pump in the manner that an ordinary installation draws heat from the air or from the ground. The heat is used to warm the building and to provide hot water. Over a period of several months, the water gets colder and colder as heat is removed. In many installations, it can get cold enough to freeze.

During summer months, the chilled water (or ice) is used to cool the air that is circulated throughout the house. The compressor of the heat pump does not have to operate during the summer.

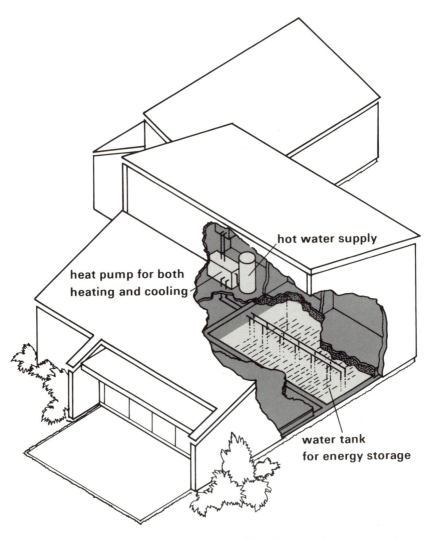

heat pump for both
heating and cooling

hot water supply

water tank
for energy storage

This is an experimental energy-cycling house. In summer heat from the house is added to the ice bin (the house is cooled). The ice melts and the water warms up.

In winter heat is taken from the water to warm the house. The water gets colder and freezes.

Only a fan to push the air is needed; also, a small pump is needed to circulate a liquid through a heat exchanger where heat from the building is picked up, and then through pipes embedded in the icy cold water where heat is removed.

Heat from the house is fed into the water, or ice, causing the temperature to rise. The tank collects the heat and holds it for use during the winter months. Year after year, heat is exchanged between the living area of the house and the tank of water in the basement—from house to water in summer; from water to house in winter. It's a case of storing up the heat of summer and using it during the cold of winter.

SOURCES OF ELECTRICITY

Electricity is the energy used to operate the compressor and the pumps that circulate air through the house. When oil is no longer available, electricity will continue to be generated in coal-burning installations for a long time. But nuclear fuel will be used more and more widely. Right now, about 12 percent of the electricity generated in the United States is nuclear. Throughout the world there are more than a hundred nuclear installations, and the number is increasing as fast as new plants can be constructed. There are many people who believe that the future will see improved fission reactors (modifications of the kind that are used now), and, eventually, fusion reactors that will produce electricity more cheaply and in larger amounts. In all likelihood, most space heating (the heating of buildings) will be electrical, and the device used will be the heat pump, in many cases solar-assisted.

In addition, the heat of the sun will be captured and used directly for space heating and for hot water. This is already being done, to a limited extent, in our country and more extensively in many other parts of the world. In Israel, 20 percent of the population heats water for their homes with solar collectors. Also, solar

University School
Media Center

energy is being harnessed to furnish hot water for hospitals, hotels, and public buildings. The annual saving amounts to more than $10 million worth of oil.

CAPTURING SOLAR ENERGY

As mentioned earlier, hot water is an expensive luxury; it accounts for about 20 percent of a home fuel bill. The cost can be decreased by the use of solar energy, which is available whenever the daytime sky is not overcast, during the summer and winter. While solar energy may not supply all the energy needed to heat water, it can fill a large part of that need.

SOLAR HOT WATER

The water in a garden hose gets very hot when it lies in the sun for an hour or two. Solar heaters are based on that idea. In latitudes where the temperature does not drop to freezing, an installation is quite simple. The main part is a heat-collecting panel: a flat box containing a flat coil of black pipes, either metal or plastic. To make the operation more efficient and to protect the equipment from the weather, the box is usually covered with a sheet of glass or plastic, and it is insulated all around. The collector is placed on a roof facing south or on the ground. It is tilted so it will receive the most direct rays of the sun for the longest part of the year. The angle of tilt varies with the latitude of the installation.

Cold water from the house system enters the collector, and warm water leaves it. The warmed water goes into the hot-water

Solar collectors on apartment houses in Israel. One third of the country's hot water for homes, offices, schools, and hospitals is supplied by solar energy. *(Consulate General of Israel in New York)*

boiler. Should it be hot enough, the water passes directly through the boiler and into the house. If the temperature needs boosting, the hot-water heater (which uses electricity, gas, or oil) turns on to raise the temperature to the desired level.

A water-filled system cannot be used in northern latitudes, for it would freeze unless it is drained. Here the solar collector is part of a system that is separate from the water supply. The system consists of a solar collector, a heat exchanger—which might be a coil inside the hot-water boiler—and a pump. The system is filled with antifreeze. Heat is transferred through the coil to the water in the boiler. An auxiliary heater in the boiler boosts the temperature higher when needed.

Systems of this kind are now available, and installation requires no unusual skills. The units are expensive, but cost will drop as more is learned about them, and as more efficient ways of making them are developed. When abundant fuel is no longer available, heaters like these will be essential; soon they will be standard equipment in new constructions.

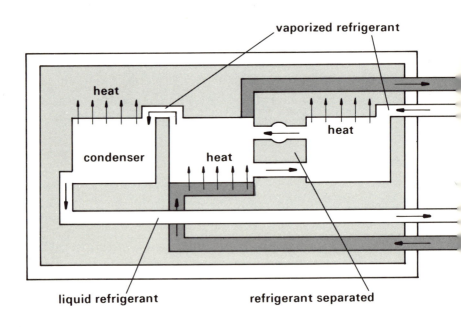

vaporized refrigerant

heat

condenser

heat

heat

liquid refrigerant

refrigerant separated

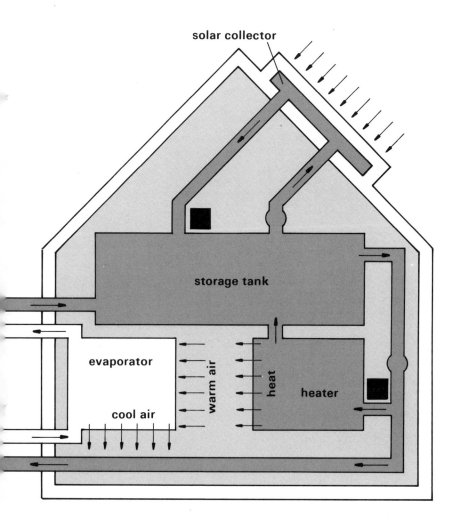

solar collector

storage tank

evaporator

warm air

heat

heater

cool air

Water is heated in the solar collector. It is piped to a storage tank. Heat from the water is used to warm the house.

In summer the hot water causes a refrigerant (now a liquid) to evaporate. This evaporation cools the house. The refrigerant (now a gas) is condensed to a liquid, releasing heat outside the house. The liquid is pumped to the evaporator, and the cycle continues.

39

The Ouroboros house at the University of Minnesota is designed to collect energy and to use it efficiently. Ouroboros was a creature from Greek mythology that survived by eating its tail, which grew constantly. *(Ouroboros South Project)*

SOLAR SPACE HEATING

When several water-filled collector panels are used, enough heat can be collected to heat hot water and also to heat the house, at least partially. The water passes through hot-water radiators in the rooms, reducing the fuel needed to bring them up to the desired temperature.

Solar-collector panels for heating air are also effective. In their simplest form, the panels are flat black boxes containing a hollow black plastic tube that is doubled back and forth from top to bottom of the collector. The boxes are well insulated, and they are covered with clear glass, or plastic. A small fan takes air from the house, or from outside, and pushes it through the plastic tube. The air moves back and forth through the length of the box, collecting

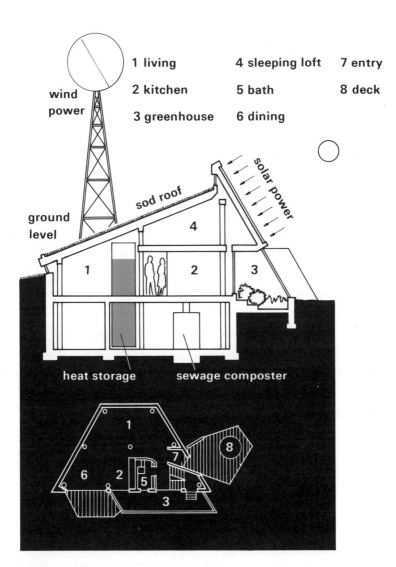

1 living   4 sleeping loft   7 entry

2 kitchen   5 bath   8 deck

3 greenhouse   6 dining

wind power

solar power

sod roof

ground level

heat storage   sewage composter

Diagram of the Ouroboros house.

Part is below ground level. Solar heat is absorbed through the windows facing south.

A greenhouse faces south. It collects energy. Large water tanks in the greenhouse hold heat during the night. In summer cool air circulates through the house. It comes in at the north and leaves at the south. A windmill with four-meter blades generates three kilowatts of electricity for heating the house when the sun is not shining.

heat as it goes. The hot air then enters the house, where it is spread into the rooms through ducts and registers. A secondary heater is connected to the system to boost the temperature when the solar heating is not sufficient to bring it to the temperature needed to be comfortable.

Solar collectors of this type are not expensive. However, a solar-heated house costs more than a conventional one. That's partly because there must be two heating systems: the usual one for nights and for those days when the sun doesn't shine, and also the solar-collecting system.

In houses, stores, hospitals, and office buildings there are many ways to reduce the fuel needed, and many of them are obvious. Make houses smaller (millions of families could get along with fewer rooms); cluster houses so several buildings can use a single heating plant; engineer buildings to save energy; and learn how to harness the energy of the sun directly for heating, as well as for generating electricity.

CONSERVING WASTE HEAT

Waste water from a bathtub or shower is usually several degrees warmer than the rest of the house. There is heat in it, yet the warm water goes into the sewer or septic system. The same thing happens with wash and rinse water from clothes washers and dishwashers.

Some builders are piping this water into a heat-exchange tank placed in front of the hot-water heater. The exchanger is usually a coil inside a tank. Heat from the water in the coil passes into the water in the tank, raising its temperature several degrees. This warmed water then goes into the hot-water heater, where the temperature is brought to the desired level. (This should not be higher than 50° C.) The cooled water then passes from the coil into the waste system.

An equally effective heat exchanger is one that transfers heat from water to air or from air to air. In this case, the coil is inside a duct through which air passes. The heat is transferred to the air as it is moved through the house. The heat in the hot air from a clothes dryer can be caught in a similar manner. The duct from the dryer now leads the hot air directly outside. With a bit of planning, the duct can be placed inside a larger one that carries air to the room. After its temperature drops, the air from the dryer can then be spilled outside the house. (Hot air contains very little heat compared to hot water at the same temperature. However, the heat should not be wasted, even though the amount may be small.)

These procedures do not reduce the amount of energy needed initially to heat the water or dry the clothes. But they do make maximum use of the heat once it is generated.

These are only suggestive of the many ways each of us can make better use of energy in our houses. No doubt others occur to you.

5 REDUCING WASTE

Living in cluster houses, driving smaller cars, getting more mileage from trucks and airplanes—these changes (and others, too) will reduce the amount of energy needed to maintain our standard of living. But all these procedures will not eliminate waste, the greatest energy-robber of all.

A little more than 5 percent of the people of the world live in the United States. But the country uses almost 35 percent of the world's supply of energy for transportation, industrial purposes, and for commercial and domestic applications.

A large part of the energy consumed is not put to use; it is wasted. Experts estimate that the amount of fuel wasted equals the amount that is imported from foreign countries. In the days when oil and gas were cheap and the supplies were almost unlimited, efficient use was not emphasized. But skyrocketing prices and rapidly increasing demands have changed all that. It is essential to use every bit of energy that is stored up in these fossil fuels.

Many European countries have had high fuel costs for decades, and they have been forced to stretch their fuel dollars. For the most part, this has been done by careful usage and by conserving fuel (oil especially) wherever possible. The western European countries have agreed that by 1985 energy consumption must be 15 percent lower than it was in 1970. Also, electricity will provide at least half of the total energy, and half of that electricity should come from nuclear power. This goal will probably not be reached by 1985, but more likely by 2000. More gas will also be used, thus reducing dependence on oil from 63 percent of the total energy requirements to less than 40 percent. In 1973 foreign oil imports (from Arabian countries for the most part) made up 98 percent of the total. By 1985 it is hoped this figure will drop to 70 percent.

In France, Germany, and England petroleum imports already have been dropping steadily. Total energy use in Germany dropped 8 percent in one year. In the same period use in the United States increased more than 5 percent, and oil imports rose more than 10 percent.

ENERGY USE IN SWEDEN

Conservation of energy is the number one requirement. In the United States we are far from realizing what can be done, as a comparison of fuel use in Sweden and the United States shows. Sweden has a much smaller population, so the total energy use is lower. However, the comparisons are per capita, that is, the energy-use per person. One way of measuring energy consumption is by relating it to the value of products produced in the country, the gross national product. The energy used in Sweden to produce each dollar of gross national product is only 60 percent of that

45

used in the United States. However, the two countries are quite
similar in their standards of living, and also in many of their
sources of income—the production of steel and other metals, of
paper, plastics, and cement.

A comparison of many aspects of the two countries is shown
below:

Table 1	U.S.	Sweden
Total degrees per person that were under 68° F, and which had to be aided by heating homes and buildings	5 500	9 200
Gross national product per person in dollars	5 000	4 500
Energy consumption per person in kilowatt hours. (Kwh are units for measuring electricity. A kwh is the amount of electricity needed to operate ten one-hundred-watt bulbs for one hour.)	98 000	60 000
Production consumption per person in kilograms		
Steel	620	680
Cement	342	430
Fertilizer	105	67
Paper	224	540

	U.S.	Sweden
Some aspects of the daily diets per person		
Energy—large calories	3 300	2 850
Protein (grams)	99	80
Cereals (g)	176	168
Meat (g)	310	142
Health and education per 1 000 persons		
Teachers	34	60
Newspapers	301	534
Books published	.39	.94
Doctors	1.50	1.35
Dentists	.49	.72
Hospital beds	7.80	15
Infant deaths	19	11
Conveniences per person		
Telephones	.59	.56
Television	.45	.32
Cars	.45	.30
Passenger miles	7 900	5 050
Percent of houses having major appliances		
Refrigerators	100	93
Freezers	28	46
Washers	76	41
Vacuums	88	89

Obviously, there are as many similarities between the two countries as there are differences. There are enough similarities to make a comparison of energy usage reasonable. Notice the large difference in energy use per capita. If these figures are broken down, the largest contrasts are in transportation, space heating of homes and commercial buildings, and industry.

Table 2
Energy Use Per Person
(in kilowatt hours)

	U.S.	Sweden
Transportation	24 000	7 700
Space heating	32 700	24 700
Industry	36 000	28 400

TRANSPORTATION

Sweden is a smaller country than the United States, therefore distances traveled are shorter. However, large amounts of the products it produces, such as paper and lumber, must be carried from the northern regions where they are obtained to the southern areas where most of the people live. Also, because the country is small, the total mileage that people drive their cars is less than the mileage driven by people in the United States—8 000 kilometers per person in Sweden against about 14 400 kilometers per person here. In driving these distances consumption in kilowatt hours for Swedish drivers is 3 760, while for U.S. drivers it is 12 630—more than three times as much. There are many reasons why the Swedish drivers use less energy, and each one of them can be applied in the United States. The most important is the weight of the cars —it accounts for about 30 percent of the difference. Cars are smaller in Sweden. The average weight is 1 100 kilograms, while in the United States the average weight is 1 700 kilograms. In addition, the engines are smaller compared to total weight. Drivers in the United States expect their cars to accelerate rapidly, climb the highest hills without downshifting, and reach speeds of 150 kilometers an hour or more. Swedish drivers have learned that such performance is not necessary for reliable and comfortable transportation. Also, for the most part, their cars do not have extras such as air conditioning and automatic transmissions, which require extra energy and so reduce gas mileage.

Not only are the cars different, but so also are the ways in which the cars are used. For short trips, which make inefficient use of fuel, the Swedes use buses and trains almost 50 percent of the time. In the United States, public transportation is used only about 10 percent of the time for short trips.

Traveling at lower speeds reduces fuel consumption. At the time these figures were assembled, only 10 percent of the highways in Sweden allowed cars to go 110 kilometers per hour, while in the United States almost all the highways allowed cars to go 105 kph. More recently, a national speed limit of 88 kph (55 mph) has been in effect in the United States. If this law were enforced, annual fuel consumption would be reduced by millions of gallons.

About 80 percent of all passenger miles are covered by cars in Sweden, while in the United States the total is a little more than 90 percent. The remaining miles are covered by public transportation. In some Swedish cities 75 percent of the commuting miles are covered by mass-transit systems and by motorbikes or bicycles. Bus and rail service is very good, and the vehicles are clean and comfortable; there are frequent departures and the cost is low.

The government has discouraged the use of private cars by

taxing them heavily. As early as 1971, the tax on gasoline was equal to fifty cents a gallon. License fees for cars go up very rapidly as the weight of the cars increases. There are also high taxes on new cars. These taxes encourage drivers to take care of their cars to make them last as long as possible. In Sweden the average life of a car is fourteen years; in the United States the average life is closer to nine years. Much energy is required to manufacture a car, so longer car life means a smaller demand for energy.

Cars are not welcome in the cities of Sweden. Limited parking is provided, and heavy fines are imposed for illegal parking. People find that it is much more convenient to travel by train or bus, and much less expensive.

Trucks that carry goods must travel greater distances in the United States than they do in Sweden. This extra distance adds a great deal to the fuel bill. However, costs can be reduced by matching the truck to the job. Where the load is small and light, and the distance is not great, the Swedes use small station wagons and so-called minitrucks that are small and light. Shippers in the United States are more apt to use heavier pickup trucks for their short hauls. It would be wise for truckers in our country to take a lesson from the Swedes and fit the job to the truck. The extra expense for buying the equipment would be recovered rapidly.

PRIVATE HOMES AND COMMERCIAL BUILDINGS

For a long time the Swedes have had expensive oil and cold winters, so they have learned how to keep heat inside their houses. They do this by good construction: joints fit tightly and there are no gaps; windows are weatherproofed all around. Instead of using one pane of glass, the Swedes use two, with dead-air space between

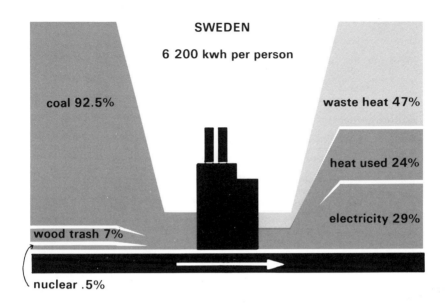

SWEDEN

6 200 kwh per person

coal 92.5%

wood trash 7%

nuclear .5%

waste heat 47%

heat used 24%

electricity 29%

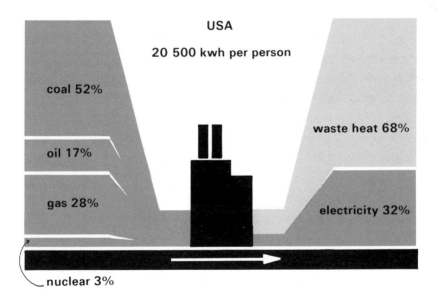

USA

20 500 kwh per person

coal 52%

oil 17%

gas 28%

nuclear 3%

waste heat 68%

electricity 32%

Generation of electricity in Sweden and the United States by the
burning of fuels.

them, or a vacuum. Storm sashes are placed over these double windows. In some newer constructions the windows are triple-paned. Also, wherever possible, the buildings face south to catch sunlight. Fewer windows are set into the north·walls, and the windows there are smaller. Where the design allows it, the windows are built only as light sources; they are not meant to be opened; therefore they are sealed tightly.

Swedish homes are also well insulated. There are at least four inches of insulation in the walls and twelve inches in the attic. Most of the homes built in the United States since about 1950 contain some insulation. There may be none in the walls, however. Very likely, only the attic floor is insulated, and even there the thickness is not enough to significantly reduce heat loss. A recent comparison of average homes in Sweden and the United States showed that the heat loss in Swedish homes was only half as great.

Individual families in Sweden use less energy for other needs as well. For example, there are fewer clothes dryers, and fewer large frost-free refrigerators. (A refrigerator/freezer that is completely frost-free runs for about 70 percent of the time—almost 18 out of 24 hours. It uses almost three times as much energy as does the same size unit that is not frost-free.) In the United States people have an electric appliance for just about every imaginable purpose —sharpening pencils, making yogurt, edging lawns, glueing—you name it.

The heating of water is a big energy user. The amount consumed for this purpose is a bit less in Sweden than in the United States, primarily because of centralized systems. In these installations the hot water comes from a boiler that may serve several single-family units, somewhat like the cluster housing mentioned earlier. Also, many apartments in Sweden are now on separate meters. When electricity, heat, or hot water is paid for as part of the rent, usage is about 15 percent higher than when each household has a separate meter. People use less energy when they must pay for it directly. Many apartments in our country are now equipped so the renter pays these costs, and consumption is lower wherever this has been done.

In commercial buildings the total use of energy in Sweden is about 70 percent of what it is in the United States. The reasons are much the same as those for private homes: solid construction and heavy insulation. In addition, the buildings use lower light levels. In the United States many commercial buildings are so well lighted that air conditioners must be used to get rid of the heat generated by the light fixtures; the heat becomes uncomfortably high.

INDUSTRIAL USE OF ENERGY

Factories that make things and assembly plants that put things together require energy for processing materials, as well as for hot water and space heating.

The paper industry in Sweden employs a good many people, and it requires large amounts of heat. Sixty percent of the energy it needs comes from the burning of the bark of trees and combustible liquids recovered from the wood itself. (In the United States paper industry, about 35 percent of the energy needed comes from these sources.)

Industries that have no waste products from which energy can be obtained can save large amounts, however. A few years ago a car-assembly plant in Sweden made a careful study of their use of energy and ways that it could be saved. They were using energy to heat the building, for hot water, for processing (drying paints, for example), and for lighting. Engineers found that there were many "leaks." Ways were found to reduce them, and the workers tried hard to be as energy-efficient as possible. After the campaign, energy use in the plant had dropped almost 30 percent. Since then, other industrial plants have reduced their energy needs by similar amounts. And the total energy usage per person in Sweden shows how effective the cuts have been.

The Swedish people enjoy a high standard of living. They have comfortable homes, cars, many have vacation houses, most have four weeks paid vacations every year; they have good schools and hospitals—and many of them. And they have all this on a relatively small amount of energy per person.

DISTRICT HEATING

In large cities of the United States, the heat for many of the buildings comes from a district heating plant. The heat is carried to the buildings in steam pipes buried underground. Much of the steam comes directly from electric turbines.

Almost all European countries have district heating systems in large cities, as well as in many smaller communities. The systems are extensively developed in Sweden, where they meet 25 percent of the total demand for space heat and for water heat; in Denmark, the total is about 32 percent; in West Germany, about 20 percent. It is used in many eastern European countries as well. The heat is transported to buildings and to individual houses through hot-water pipes rather than steam pipes, as in the United States. They are buried underground, much as the sewage system. Smaller pipes connect each house to the main system. Transporting the heat via water is better than steam because pipes that carry steam are more expensive than those that carry water, and are more apt to break down. Maintenance of steam pipes is expensive. When water is used, the temperature can be lower than steam—a bit under 100° C is sufficient; and the water can be transported over distances of several kilometers without losing too much heat.

Costs in many of the European installations are kept low because waste heat is used. Fuel is not burned only to obtain the heat. The heat comes from many sources, but mainly from electric generating plants. Coal or nuclear fuels produce hot steam to operate turbines that are connected to electric generators. When the steam leaves the turbine, its temperature drops, but it is still very hot. About 70 percent of the energy in the steam is not converted to electricity; it is wasted up the chimney or discarded through a cooling tower. In the European installations, this heat goes into a heat exchanger where water is heated, and the hot water goes into the district heating system. Nuclear-electric generators, which are widely used, produce more heat than the turbines can use, and excess heat is removed from the reactor itself. The heat raises the temperature of the water that circulates through the district heating system. In nuclear stations there is no loss of heat up a chimney, for there is no combustion, as with coal or oil. This factor, together with devices to prevent heat losses all along the way, makes it possible to reach almost 95 percent efficiency. This means that 95 percent of the potential heat in the fuel is used —only 5 percent is wasted.

Other sources of waste heat exist, though the supply is not as great as that from electric generating plants, nor is it as steady. Certain industries, such as steel and the processing of other metals, produce waste heat that is fed into the system. Another possibility that is being developed is the burning of refuse. Not only can this provide heat, but it also offers a solution to the problem of waste disposal. The garbage produced in a United States city having an average climate can be turned into enough heat to fill

7 or 8 percent of the energy needed for space and water heating.

There are many reasons why district heating is more common in Europe than in our own country. One is that fuel has been cheaper here; therefore, the need to develop the plan was not urgent. In Europe, fuels have been expensive for many years; the people had to find alternatives. With the rapidly increasing costs of coal and oil, people in our country will consider district heating more seriously.

The cost of installation is high. About the only way of meeting the cost is through government support, as is done with the installation of most sewage systems. Also, the hot-water lines may cross from town to town, from city to city, and from state to state. Therefore, the federal government must be involved.

Problems of cost and sometimes conflicting interests of local governments can be solved. The important thing is to make full use of fuels and to reduce waste wherever possible. District heating increases the efficiency of every steam-generating electric plant, no matter what the fuel, be it coal, oil, gas, or nuclear. It increases the efficiency of industrial operations that now waste much of the heat that they generate, largely from the burning of coal and oil. And district heating is a reasonable way of putting to use the energy that we throw away each day in our garbage and trash.

New housing should be designed for district heating. As sewer lines are put in, so also should hot-water lines. Established towns should consider seriously how waste heat from generating plants in the area can be piped into their homes.

Without changing the standard of living, energy consumption in the United States could be cut 30 percent. It can be done by driving smaller cars, driving less, using trains and buses, insulating buildings, installing district heating, and by using waste heat from electric generating stations.

6 ENERGY ALTERNATIVES: ELECTRICITY

Civilization will not end when gas and oil are depleted. And, hopefully, people of the world will not face calamities such as those described in the first chapter. Discoveries and inventions not even dreamed about today will probably have been made by that time. New methods of dealing with the energy dilemma may be developed. Surely, ways of mining, transporting, and burning coal efficiently and economically will be found. And many believe that nuclear fusion will be controlled and usable early in the twenty-first century.

For most applications electricity is the most convenient form of energy. It can be conducted anywhere via wires and cables. At the consuming location, electricity can be converted easily to light, heat, motion—whatever one requires, and without producing any pollution. Throughout the world small amounts of electricity are being generated by falling water or by solar-electric cells. By far the largest amount of electricity (about 93 percent) is generated

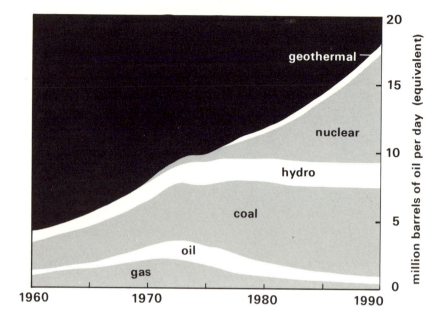

In the years ahead use of oil for generating electricity will decrease. There will be large increases in the use of coal and nuclear energy.

by turbines. Nuclear energy drives some of them, but for the most part they are driven by the heat from coal, oil, and gas. At the close of the 1970's, about 52 percent of the plants burned coal, and 45 percent used either oil or gas.

COAL

There is much more coal in the world than oil and gas, but oil and gas are more readily available. They are cheaper to obtain, cheaper to transport, and convenient to burn. Pipelines carry gas and oil to all parts of a country. The Alaska pipeline carries oil from the fields in the northern part of the state to the southern part. Here the oil is loaded on ships that transport it to the west coast of the United States. A network of pipelines carries oil and gas from the west and south to the east coast states. In Russia and the eastern Asian countries, pipelines carry oil and gas thousands of miles from the wells to refineries.

Because of the advantages of oil and gas, these fuels have been used more and more, and coal has been used less and less. Russia has been an exception; in most installations, coal is the primary fuel. Oil is reserved for special uses, not for large stationary boilers. Another factor that has affected the use of coal is pollution. Even when coal is burned thoroughly, sulfur compounds are produced. Sulfur in the coal combines with oxygen in the air to produce sulfur dioxide, a gas that is harmful to plants and animals. Other poisonous gases produced by burning coal are those made of nitrogen and oxygen (nitrogen oxides). Incidentally, these are also the principal pollutants in the exhaust fumes from cars. The amount of gaseous oxides given off by one large coal-burning plant is equal to the exhausts of 200 000 automobiles. Coal-burning plants also release benzopyrene, which is the main cancer-causing substance in cigarettes.

Other kinds of pollution also come from coal fires. Every second, a large coal-burning power plant pushes 600 pounds of carbon dioxide into the atmosphere. The gas in itself is not harmful. However, it is believed that large amounts in the atmosphere may affect the climate of the world. The carbon dioxide could act as a blanket around the earth, preventing heat from escaping. An increase of three or four degrees in average temperature would be enough to melt snow and ice in arctic regions and in mountain glaciers. The level of the oceans would be raised several feet, enough to flood major cities of the world.

Unless very expensive scrubbers (devices to clean out the combustion products) are installed in the chimneys, coal-burning also

59

releases tiny particles into the air. Because of their small size, the particles do not settle out; they are held in the air. The particles inhaled into the body enter the lungs, where they are deposited. Accumulations could lead to lung irritations and respiratory problems.

When coal is burned, there is also an accumulation of ashes. A large plant produces thirty pounds of ashes per second. Disposal of them is often a problem.

Hopefully, as our skills improve, ways will be found to reduce pollutants from coal fires, and so remove one of the barriers to increased usage.

No one knows precisely how much coal there is. Figures vary, but conservative estimates indicate there's enough coal to last three hundred years at our present level of energy demands, and there may be enough for a thousand years. Russia has just as much coal reserves as the United States, perhaps a great deal more. But, as it happens, most of the coal in the United States and Russia is not where it is needed. It is in out-of-the-way places where population is low, and so energy demands are low. Also, much of the coal is low-grade; there are many impurities that have to be removed before the coal is usable.

In some areas the coal is near the surface. It is dug out of the ground by huge steam shovels. Entire countrysides are picked up and carried away to plants that process the coal. The coal is often put into railroad cars that carry it to the plants where it is washed and pulverized. The powdered coal then can be mixed with water and carried through pipelines, much as oil is transported. At the electric generating plant, the water is removed, and the powdered coal is sprayed into a boiler where it burns completely.

The cost of mining coal, removing impurities, and transporting it will continue to be high. And the cost will be increased because land destroyed by mining operations must be made productive

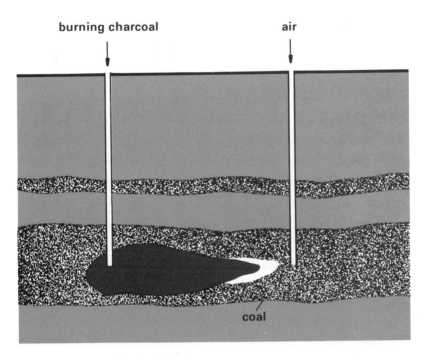

burning charcoal   air

coal

Coal may be gasified by heating it under the ground. Two wells are dug. A charcoal fire is dropped down the well at the left, and air is pumped down the well at the right. The coal is not packed solid, so it is able to burn toward the air. By controlling the amount of air, the coal burns only partially. The unburned gas is removed through the left well.

again. But the cost of gas and oil will be even higher, so we can expect to see coal used more and more in the generating of electricity.

Before any fuel burns, it must be turned into a gas. The flames from a wood fire are the burning gases that the heat drives out of the wood. In a gasoline engine, gasoline is atomized and combined with air. It is the gasoline-air mixture that ignites in the cylinders. An oil burner sprays droplets of oil into air (oxygen), and it's this gaseous mixture that ignites.

In some areas the coal is changed to a gas at the mine. The gas can then be sent through pipelines to a generating plant.

Coal can also be used to make gasoline. This was done extensively in Germany during World War II. The process was extremely expensive, much too costly for it to be practical in peacetime. However, South Africa is now producing 25 percent of its gasoline from coal. In this case, the operation is practical because coal can be mined and processed very cheaply in South Africa.

In spite of all the problems, we can expect that the use of coal for generating electricity and perhaps for making gasoline will increase. In the next few decades, coal will probably become the transition fuel from gas and oil to nuclear-electric power.

NUCLEAR FUEL

Presently, more and more of the world's electricity is generated by nuclear fuel. The percentage will become greater in the years ahead, perhaps reaching 50 percent by the year 2000. All of Japan's oil is imported, and almost two-thirds of its coal. The country must develop nuclear energy, and it is doing so right now. The urgency is shown by the time required to build a plant—in Japan, three and a half years elapse between the decision to build and operation. In the United States it takes ten years or more. There is much opposition to the building of nuclear plants, since many people connect nuclear reactors with nuclear bombs. They remember the horror of the atom bombs that were dropped on Hiroshima and Nagasaki in 1945.

Changes in consumption of Japan's energy over a thirteen-year period are shown below. Note the large increase in nuclear energy.

Table 3
Daily Energy Consumption in Japan
(equivalent to 1 000 barrels of oil)

	1972	1980	1985
Oil	4 933	7 747	9 160
Natural Gas	80	683	941
Coal	1 150	1 417	1 865
Nuclear	46	714	2 044
Hydroelectric and Geothermal	189	209	231

There is also pressure to build nuclear generators in western Europe. France, for example, will probably have twenty nuclear plants operating in the early 1980's. This is down from the fifty that were planned originally. The number has decreased because of costs—the plants are extremely expensive and are becoming more so. Also, engineers have met serious technical problems, not the least of which is disposal of waste products. Perhaps of most importance, however, is the strong public feeling against nuclear power plants. People feel they are not as safe as they should be; they fear that the plants may endanger their health by polluting the air and water. This in spite of the fact that a major accident in 1979 (at Three Mile Island in Pennsylvania) did not injure a single person.

Nuclear fuel is the cheapest by far. Nuclear plants are the most expensive to build, but the fuel they use is the least expensive. In the United States, for every thirty cents spent on oil as fuel and seventeen cents spent on coal, less than six cents is spent on nuclear fuel.

The fuel used in a nuclear reactor is uranium 235 (the number is the total of the protons (92) and neutrons (143) in the nucleus

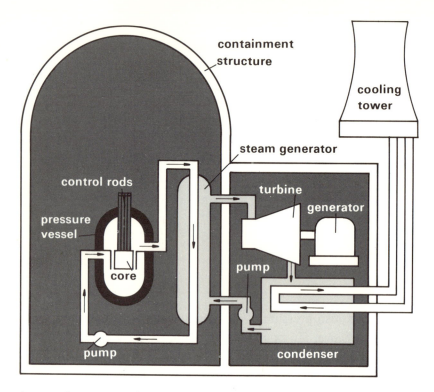

In a nuclear reactor heat produced in the reactor core is carried to a steam generator. The steam travels through a separate system to a turbine–electric generator.

of the atom). Most of the uranium is made of atoms that contain a total of 238 particles. (Natural uranium is .7 uranium 235 and 99.3 uranium 238.) Only the nucleus of an atom of uranium 235 fissions—splits apart under certain conditions and releases energy.

The reactors, of which there are close to 200 presently operating in countries around the world, are called light-water reactors. Most use ordinary water, and there are two types: boiling-water reactors and pressurized-water reactors. In both of them, the uranium fuel is enriched so it is about three percent uranium 235. This percentage is not nearly high enough to produce a nuclear explosion. Should such a reactor ever malfunction, it would not explode. Instead, there would be a rapid buildup of heat and, under the most extreme malfunction (which has never occurred anywhere), a melt-down of the core of the reactor.

The boiling-water reactor has a pressure vessel that contains fuel rods. The uranium 235 atoms are bombarded by neutrons, causing them to split. In the process, other atoms are produced, and heat is released. Water circulating around the fuel rods is changed to steam. The steam is led to a turbine that is connected to an electric generator. The steam cools somewhat, the water returns to the reactor where it picks up more heat, and the cycle continues.

The pressurized reactor is essentially the same. However, the water that circulates through the fuel rods is pressurized; it does not change to steam. The hot pressurized water passes through an exchanger, where its heat is transferred to another and separate water system. Steam generated in this system drives a turbine generator in the usual fashion.

Fuel rods remain in the reactors for three or four years. Each year a percentage of them are replaced. The old rods contain waste products that slow down the fission process, much as ashes smother a fire. These rods are usually stored underground.

Nuclear reactors produce very little waste. Let's consider a large installation, one that generates as much electricity as a large coal-burning plant. Only two cubic meters of wastes would be produced in a whole year. These wastes are radioactive, that is, they give off harmful radiation. The most energetic radiation is in the form of gamma rays. After processing to remove the useful uranium, the wastes will be stored underground in salt domes— hollow caves in salt deposits. These deposits are geologically stable, that is, they do not shift, and they are not apt to be affected by earthquakes. The wastes will be placed 600 meters below the surface, and they will remain there for centuries.

When, and if, all electricity in the United States is generated by nuclear fission (which is most unlikely), the annual waste from all the reactors would occupy an area that is less than half a square kilometer. (Nuclear fusion reactors, which are discussed later, are even more free of waste products—they are completely pollution-free.)

No one knows how much uranium there is on this planet of ours. No doubt, there are many deposits that have not been discovered. However, estimates have been made indicating how long the supply will last. The most pessimistic experts say that nuclear reactors of the kind now in operation will be able to function only a few decades. Others say a hundred years. The more optimistic estimates indicate there's enough fuel to last six or seven hundred years. Time will tell. Meanwhile, other and longer-lasting types of reactors are being studied and built experimentally in the United States, England, France, Russia, Germany, Japan, and Italy.

BREEDER REACTORS

Light-water reactors are also called slow reactors because the neutrons are slowed down. Hydrogen in the water molecules decelerates them. These slow-moving neutrons are able to split uranium 235 nuclei; only occasionally do they enter the uranium 238 nucleus.

Breeder reactors also produce heat. But, at the same time, they make plutonium 239 from uranium 238—and plenty of it, for, you recall, 99 percent of uranium is uranium 238. Plutonium is also fissionable. The wonder of these reactors is that they breed more fuel than they consume. Therefore, fuel supplies can continue almost endlessly for centuries to come.

A breeder reactor starts with a small amount of plutonium as

stairwell indicates scale

containment structure

A active core   C primary sodium circuit   E water steam
B breeding blanket   D secondary sodium circuit   circuit

Superphenix is a breeder reactor—it produces energy and also breeds (produces) plutonium, which is additional fuel. This is an overhead view.

a fuel. Fission of the plutonium provides heat. It also provides the neutrons that are captured by the uranium 238 nuclei, which initiates the changes that result in the making of more plutonium.

The reactor core contains liquid sodium, a substance that does not slow down neutrons. The sodium picks up heat, and it also becomes radioactive. For safety purposes, the heat is transferred to a second closed sodium circuit, which is not radioactive. This hot liquid sodium goes to a heat exchanger that contains water. The water is changed to steam, and the steam pushes a turbine generator.

At the moment several of these reactors are test-operating in many countries. A commercial installation has been working in Russia since the late 1960's. Superphenix, a French reactor that will generate over a million kilowatts of electricity, will be located in the countryside about forty kilometers from Lyon.

Plutonium is a highly radioactive substance, and small amounts of it can be lethal. Therefore, the metal must be handled with great care. Also, relatively small amounts of plutonium can be fashioned into an explosive charge and made into a bomb. There's a possibility that wrongdoers could seize and hold the plutonium, using it to threaten the rest of the world. Because of possible dangers of this kind, some countries, notably the United States, are moving very slowly with breeder reactors. However, other people point out that these reactors hold so much promise that their potential should be explored energetically. Assuming that forecasts of the uranium reserves are correct, breeder reactors could supply energy for a thousand years. Ordinary reactors that use only the uranium 235 nuclei at best will fill the energy needs for no more than a few hundred years.

FUSION REACTORS

The energy of the sun comes from nuclear fusion: the joining together of the nuclei of hydrogen to produce helium. The reaction occurs at the core of the sun where the temperature is at least 14 million degrees. Engineers are now attempting to create this reaction on the earth. The experimental device, being developed

Tokamaks are devices designed to control nuclear fusion—the process that might furnish an endless supply of energy for the entire world. *(General Atomic Company)*

at Princeton University, is called tokamak, after the Russian installation, the first of its kind. When scientists learn how to do this and how to control the reaction, engineers will have solved the energy needs of the world. Hydrogen in the waters of the oceans will become the basic fuel. In every gallon of sea water there's

69

one-eighth of a gram of deuterium (heavy hydrogen that is a combined proton and neutron). This tiny amount of matter contains as much energy as 1 100 liters of gasoline. There's enough deuterium in the oceans to supply all our energy for billions of years, even if the present demand should increase a hundred times.

Critical and basic problems in controlled nuclear fusion are containment—how to hold together the reacting materials for the required fraction of time—and how to prevent the container from melting down because of the high temperature, or from flying apart before the reaction is completed.

These are frontiers that are being explored right now. Engineers say that progress is being made, but slowly. Some say that it will take another forty or fifty years before we learn enough to tame the fusion reaction. Others say we may have a breakthrough by 1990, if not earlier.

Scientists in England, Russia, Japan, France, and the United States are seeking ways to start and control continous nuclear fusion. To do so, they must get the material to a very high temperature on the order of 100 million degrees, to densities as high as 100 trillion particles per cubic centimeter, and hold the reacting materials together for at least half a second. That gets the reaction started. Once that is accomplished, there is the problem of containing the materials so the reaction will continue, therefore producing more energy than has been put into the system.

The sequence of nuclear-energy development may go somewhat like this: Right now, and in the years immediately ahead, light-water reactors will meet more and more of the world's energy needs. At the same time, breeder-reactor technology will increase. Gradually, fast breeders will replace the light-water reactors. This will carry us into the twenty-first century. A few decades into that century, and perhaps much earlier, fusion reactors will be operating. A virtually endless supply of energy will then be available.

ELECTRICITY TO HYDROGEN ENERGY

The fossil-fuel age is at best a short interval in man's existence. We began to use coal, oil, and gas in rapidly increasing quantities about 1850. Judging by present indications, these fuels will be phased out by the year 2350 (some even say by 2050—within the lifetimes of many people now living). Two centuries (or five, for that matter) is little more than a moment in the million years and more that people have been on this planet.

Eventually, most, if not all, of the world's supply of energy will be in the form of electricity. Nuclear fusion will supply most of it but the total will come from many sources:

Source of Electricity	Operation and Present Status
Slow light-water reactors	Now operating worldwide.
Fast breeder reactors	Experimental, although operating in some countries.
Nuclear fusion reactors	Research, perhaps a breakthrough by 1990.
Solar cells	Now operating for special uses, such as satellites, weather stations, telephone relays.
Solar thermal units	Generating steam with experimental mirrors that focus heat onto boilers. Very costly at present.
Geothermal	Using steam from below surface to drive turbines. Now used on small scale, in Iceland and California.

Source of Electricity	Operation and Present Status
Wind power	Used on small scale. Research on large installations.
Hydroelectric power	Harnessing all waterfalls, even those far from cities.
Solar sea power	Driving generators with temperature differences between hot, tropical surface water and cooler water at lower depths. Experimental.
Tides	Harnessing tidal movements of sea water to operate turbine generators. Working in France.
Photosynthesis	Growing crops to produce fuels to drive turbines. Research being conducted.
Organic wastes	Processing garbage and sewage to recover fuels for operating turbines. Now operating in many places.

It's entirely possible that within a few decades these various sources will produce electricity in such quantities that there will be an ample supply for everyone and at an affordable price. Most of the electricity will be used directly, as it now is. However, this will be true only where the installations are fairly close to the places where the electricity is needed. Because there is such a high loss when electricity is sent over long distances, the electricity will be "stored" in containers at the generating plant. Electricity will

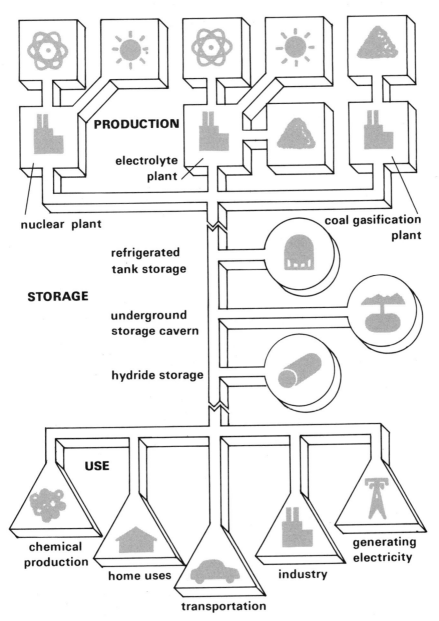

PRODUCTION

electrolyte plant

nuclear plant

coal gasification plant

STORAGE

refrigerated tank storage

underground storage cavern

hydride storage

USE

chemical production

home uses

transportation

industry

generating electricity

Someday hydrogen may be the main fuel for the whole world. It may be produced in nuclear plants, solar collectors, and from coal. The hydrogen may be stored in tanks, in caverns underground, or as compounds (hydrides) of hydrogen. Hydrogen can be used directly (burned with oxygen), or it can be used to generate electricity.

break water molecules apart into the hydrogen and oxygen of which they are made. The energy that was in the electricity will now be contained in the hydrogen and oxygen.

The gases will be liquefied and transported in tanks to wherever they are needed. Very likely, the hydrogen, which is explosive and hazardous to handle, will be combined with nitrogen to make ammonia (NH_3), or with metals to make hydrides, as explained earlier. It can be handled more easily in these forms and can later be taken out of the molecules with relative economy.

At the location where it is to be used, the hydrogen could be burned with oxygen. This produces a large amount of heat for operating turbine generators, as well as water as an end product. The energy stored in the gases is set free—the electricity generated at one location is made available at another location far removed. Or, the hydrogen could be used to activate fuel cells. These, you recall, produce electricity directly with water as the only other product.

Some of you reading this book will be around when mankind enters the age of electricity. It will be a period of endless energy for the entire world.

A NONNUCLEAR FUTURE

The energy-rich future described above assumes that engineers will continue to develop generators powered by nuclear energy, for it seems that nuclear fusion reactors hold the most promise for supplying large amounts of electricity over long periods of time. Much activity throughout the world is aimed at this objective, as discussed earlier.

Not everyone is confident that nuclear energy will succeed—or that it should. These people argue against developing nuclear energy. Some of the arguments are reasonable, but others show that they don't understand nuclear energy. For example, many people say they will not use nuclear electricity because the electricity will be contaminated. The idea is ridiculous, of course. Electricity has no properties that are dependent upon the way it is generated; all electricity is the same in that respect. The fear arises from connections that these people make between nuclear energy and nuclear bombs.

A nuclear reactor is not explosive, because the concentration of fuel is far below the critical level. However, a reactor can become extremely hot. There are numerous controls that keep the reaction at a safe level, or shut down the operation if, for any reason, the activity goes too fast. If the controls did not function, the reactor would overheat. In fact, it would produce so much heat that the core of the reactor, and surrounding installations, would melt down. The level of nuclear radiation would rise, but it would be contained within the outer protective barriers.

Another concern of antinuclear thinking is radiation, which may cause cancer and injure the cells of plants and animals in other ways as well. When a reactor operates, it produces waste products, some of which are radioactive. Many of them have half-lives of several hundred, or thousands of, years. (A half-life of a thousand years means that it takes that long for one-half of any given amount to lose its radioactivity.) Radioactive waste products from the more than one hundred reactors now operating are buried in underground pits from which they may be removed at some time in the future. Underground locations 600 meters below the earth's surface are now being engineered for permanent burial of these waste products. Breeder reactors, discussed earlier, use much of their own waste, utilizing it to generate additional energy.

75

Antinuclear groups believe that the future of mankind must not be based on the development of nuclear-electric energy. They feel that as gas and oil disappear, there must be a decrease in the demands for energy. The demands such as they are will be met by using solar energy. In addition, many other sources will be utilized, as listed on pages 71–72. There will still be burnable fuels for special uses, fuels obtained from plants or, as they are often called, renewable biologic materials.

Some engineers say that electricity will become less important with the passage of time. In fact, they say the only need for it will be for lighting, for operating electric motors, and for various kinds of electronic equipment. If so, that would amount to only about 10 percent of present usage. It is an amount that could be produced by solar installations, windmill systems, and hydroelectric installations.

Even so, burnable fuels would still be needed for transportation. These fuels would come from the fermentation of crops—wheat, oats, barley, malt, hops, rice—and the generation of alcohol. Presently, the beer, wine, and liquor industry is based upon the fermentation process. Make the processing plants larger, it is argued, and there would be enough alcohol to run cars and trucks. At the same time, we must make cars smaller and lighter, and use smaller trucks wherever possible.

Electric generating stations that also provide heat for buildings in the area might operate by using alcohol, although the demand would be tremendous, and it's difficult to imagine how so much alcohol could be produced. However, coal would still be used as well, since the supply may be sufficient to last several hundred years. Instead of there being huge generating stations for a large area that includes scores of communities, each small region would have its own station. It's argued that in these smaller installations more of the cost goes into electricity at the point of use. Less is lost in transmitting the electricity to substations and distributing it to individual users. Perhaps people will learn to adjust to less energy, but the prospect is not realistic. People resist strongly any decrease in their standard of living; they hope to make it better. As decades go by, resistance to the development of energy sources (especially coal and nuclear) will decrease, and rapid progress will be made.

No one can say when it will happen. But, eventually, there will be no oil or gas, and even coal reserves will be depleted. The fossil-fuel age will end.

Now is the time to plan our energy future, one that will see a rapid decrease in the use of fossil fuels. And now is the time to work on plans that will take us smoothly from the fossil-fuel age to the age of electricity. Each of us can conserve energy. Each of us can support research efforts to find ways of living that demand smaller amounts of energy to stretch the dwindling oil supply. The search for new energy sources must also be encouraged. We must discover economical ways to make high-grade liquid fuel from coal and from plants, how to use solar energy widely and economically, and how to make possible a hydrogen-electric economy. Alternatively, an entirely revolutionary fuel technology may be invented, one that no one has yet considered. Judging by the progress in technology of many kinds made since 1950, we can expect exciting developments during the last quarter of this century. Certainly, we have not reached the point where inventions or discoveries will cease. But we cannot sit idly by and wait for inventors to invent. Tomorrow is the future—it can be a time of abundant energy.

FURTHER READINGS

Adler, Irving. *Energy.* New York: John Day, 1970.

Branley, Franklyn M. *Energy for the 21st Century.* New York: Thomas Y. Crowell, 1975.

Clark, Wilson. *Energy for Survival: The Alternative to Extinction.* Garden City, N.Y.: Anchor Press, 1974.

Considine, Douglas M., ed. *Energy Technology Handbook.* New York: McGraw-Hill, 1977.

Doty, Roy. *Where Are You Going with That Energy?* Chicago Museum of Science and Industry Series. New York: Doubleday, 1977.

Gulf Oil Corporation. *An Eagle Eye on Energy.* Houston: Gulf Oil Corporation, n.d.

Halacy, D. S., Jr. *Earth, Water, Wind, and Sun: Our Energy Alternatives.* New York: Harper & Row, Publishers, 1977.

————.*The Energy Trap.* New York: Four Winds Press, 1975.

Hand, A. J. *Home Energy How-To.* A Popular Science Book. New York: Harper & Row, Publishers, 1977.

Hayes, Denis. *Energy for Development: Third World Options.* Worldwatch Paper no. 15. Washington, D.C.: Worldwatch Institute, 1977.

Kaplan, William and Lebowitz, Melvyn. *Energy and Fuels.* Student Scientist Series. New York: Rosen, 1976.

National Science Teachers Association. *Factsheets on Alternative Energy Technologies.* Washington, D.C.: National Science Teachers Association, 1977. Distributed by U.S. Department of Energy.

Pringle, Laurence. *Energy: Power for People.* New York: Macmillan, 1975.

Rothman, Milton A. *Energy and the Future.* New York: Franklin P. Watts, 1975.

Sheridan, David and Gordon, Irene S. *Alternative Energy Sources.* Vital Issues Series. Washington, Conn.: Center for Information on America, 1975.

Sierra Club. *Energy Packet.* San Francisco: Sierra Club Information Services, n.d.

United States Executive Office of the President, Energy Policy and Planning. *The National Energy Plan.* Washington, D.C.: U.S. Government Printing Office, 1977. Distributed by U.S. Department of Energy, Technical Information Center.

Wilson, Mitchell. *Energy.* Rev. ed. Life Science Library. Morristown, N.J.: Time-Life Books, 1970.

Woodburn, John H. *Energy.* Merit Badge Pamphlet no. 3335. North Brunswick, N.J.: Boy Scouts of America, 1978.

INDEX

Page entries in *italics* refer to illustrations

ABOUT THE AUTHOR

Franklyn M. Branley, Astronomer Emeritus and former Chairman of The American Museum-Hayden Planetarium, is well known as the author of many books about astronomy and other sciences for young people of all ages. He is also co-editor of the Let's-Read-and-Find-Out Science Books.

Dr. Branley holds degrees from New York University, Columbia University, and the State University of New York College at New Paltz. He and his wife live in Sag Harbor, New York.

ABOUT THE ILLUSTRATOR

Henry Roth is a photographer and graphic designer. He has produced television commercials, and he both produced and directed an educational film and a film for New York's Joffrey Ballet. His meticulous illustrations have appeared in several science books. This is the third book by Franklyn M. Branley he has illustrated.

Mr. Roth was born in Cleveland, Ohio, and received his degree from the Cleveland Institute of Art. He now lives in New York City.